Cooking in the Nude

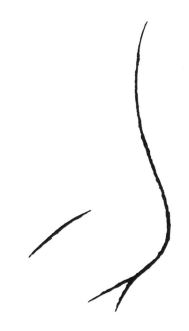

Just Married

Designed by Carolyn Weary Brandt
Edited by Keri Moser

Printed in Canada
Published by Howell Press, Inc., 1147 River Road, Suite 2,
Charlottesville, Virginia 22901.
Telephone (804) 977-4006
First Printing

HOWELL PRESS

Publisher's Cataloging in Publication
(Prepared by Quality Books Inc.)

Cornwell, Debbie.
  Cooking in the nude : just married / Debbie Cornwell, Stephen
Cornwell. -- Rev., expanded ed.
  p. cm.
  Includes index.

  1. Cookery. 2. Cookery for two. 3. Honeymoons. I. Cornwell,
Stephen L. II. Title.

TX714.C67 1997   641.5
                          QBI97-40106

TABLE OF CONTENTS

INTRODUCTION

JUST MARRIED . . .
is the playful and romantic approach to gourmet dining for newlyweds. Whether you've just tied the knot, or plan to soon, you're sure to enjoy the fun and romance of JUST MARRIED.

CONGRATULATIONS!
We wish you all the best, but before you prepare your first romantic recipe, we encourage you to read each chapter! Be sure you understand the real "Facts of Life" before you even think of experimenting with "Unbridaled Passions!" And please make certain your partner appreciates the importance of the "Undress Rehearsals" before going "Over the Threshold" together!

BON VOYAGE!
We think you'll find the elegant, yet easy, recipes in JUST MARRIED will launch your new life together with fun and style . . . may the honeymoon never end!

THE FACTS OF LIFE
(Creating the Mood)

*N*ow that you're married, you owe it to yourselves to understand all the facts of life! Sure, Mom and Dad told you a lot, but there were a few things even your best friends couldn't share. They knew you had to be there first!

For example, let's look at the real facts about romance and passion. Someone once said that passions are like fires; they go out if left unattended. But the romance doesn't ever have to end if you keep the temperature hot enough! It's all a matter of creating (and maintaining) the right mood. And we think that using the dining room as a prelude to the bedroom is one of the most fun and stimulating ways to keep a sizzling relationship going long after your return from the honeymoon!

But how can you make it happen? You've moved into your new home and gone back to work. Even before you've had time to exchange the last wedding present, you're beginning to establish the usual patterns and routines of a new household. Yes, you both work hard, there never seems to be enough time, and cooking can become a chore. But don't resign yourself to the typical tasteless dinnertime routine. How many times a week can "Halibut Helper" or a frozen "Gourmet Whatever" turn you on? And while Macaroni and Cheese has its place, it's not one of the top ten aphrodisiacs! Even if you go out often for an intimate candlelight dinner, you'll encounter your share of mediocre meals, poor service, and bad tables, all of which may dampen the fires of romance for the evening.

So what's the solution? From the beginning, set aside one night a week (two is even more fun) for a playful Epicurean rendezvous at home! Heighten and excite your lover's libido by creating a simple, yet sensuous, dining experience. You don't need exotic ingredients or complex recipes to accomplish your romantic goal. Just avoid conversations about work, in-laws, and money. Focus on the topics you both enjoyed during courtship and leave the phone off the hook. It's a simple romantic recipe and one of the most fun facts of life!

BOUQUETS AND GARTERS
(Presentation)

*I*n the wedding ceremony the bridal veil suggests mystique, the bouquet adds an air of innocence, and the garter provides a glimpse of things to come! Just as every element of the bride's attire contributes to the romance of the day, so must each part of your table setting enhance the passionate purpose of the evening that lies ahead.

After all, you've been in a state of (shall we say) anticipation all day! Tonight, you've selected a most tempting and provocative menu, intended to fulfill your every desire! To accomplish your goal, you now need to enhance its presentation to the hilt by utilizing all those wonderful (although sometimes gaudy) wedding presents to their fullest potential!

Don't become like so many married couples who only bring out the "good" china and the sterling candle holders twice a year for "special" occasions. We ask, what could be more special than a romantic romp with your sweetheart tonight? And, if you actually use the Wedgwood (or whatever) once a week, it won't be long before the mere sight of the pattern has your partner panting for veils and garters and everything in between.

What a pleasurable routine to fall into! As someone once said, "too much of a good thing can be wonderful!"

SUGAR AND SPICE

(Pantry Needs)

*S*ugar and spice make everything nice, and tonight your true love you'll surely entice!

Enticing entrées are easy to create when you have all the right ingredients. A supply of the following herbs, spices, and spirits will allow you to indulge in all of our romantic recipes! All herbs and spices are dried unless otherwise noted.

♥ ♥ ♥ ♥ ♥ ♥ ♥ ♥ ♥ ♥ ♥ ♥ ♥ ♥ ♥ ♥ ♥

All-purpose flour
Almonds
Artichoke hearts
   packed in water
Balsamic vinegar
Basil
Bay leaves
Black olives
Bourbon
Brandy
Brown sugar
Burgundy
Capers
Caraway seeds
Cayenne
Chili sauce
Chopped, peeled
   tomatoes
Chutney (fig-based,
   if available)
Cider vinegar
Cinnamon
Coffee
Cognac
Coriander
Cornstarch
Crackers

Currants
Dijon mustard
Dill
Dry mustard
Dry white wine
   (Sauternes, if available)
Fennel seed
Fines herbes
Garlic powder
Garlic salt
Grated lemon peel
Grated orange peel
Ground cloves
Ground ginger
Honey
Ketchup
Madeira
Marinated artichoke
   crowns
Marjoram
Marsala
Nutmeg
Olive oil
Onion powder
Oregano
Paprika
Pecans

Peppercorns
Pine nuts
Port
Poultry seasoning
Prepared mustard
Raisins
Raspberry vinegar
Red wine vinegar
Rice
Rosemary
Salt
Sherry
Shortening
Soy sauce
Sugar
Tabasco sauce
Tarragon
Thyme
Tomato juice
Tomato paste
Turmeric
Vegetable oil
Vermouth
Walnuts
White pepper
White vinegar
Worcestershire sauce

Escargot in Caps

25 minutes

Step One:

1/2 cup butter, room temperature
2 Tbsp. chopped fresh parsley
2 cloves garlic, minced
1 tsp. minced onion
salt and pepper to taste
pinch nutmeg

Blend butter with remaining ingredients.

Step Two:

juice of 1/2 lemon
24 medium mushrooms, stems
 removed
2 7-oz. cans escargot, rinsed and
 drained

Preheat oven to 350°F. Squeeze lemon juice over mushroom caps. Place a dab of seasoned butter in each cap. Place one escargot in each cap. Cover each escargot with remaining seasoned butter and place on baking sheet or escargot plates. Heat in oven until butter bubbles.

Hot 'n' Sweet

15 minutes

Step One:

1 15-oz. can pineapple chunks in
 heavy syrup
1/2 cup firmly packed brown sugar
1/4 cup lemon juice
2 Tbsp. cornstarch
1 tsp. prepared mustard

Drain and reserve syrup from pineapple. Combine syrup and all remaining ingredients, except pineapple chunks, in small saucepan. Stir over medium heat until thickened.

Step Two:

2 cups cubed ham
pineapple chunks

Add ham and pineapple chunks to pan. Stir until hot. Serve with toothpicks.

Cream Cheese Ball

40 minutes

Step One:

1 8-oz. pkg. cream cheese, softened
1 Tbsp. mayonnaise
1/2 tsp. Worcestershire
1 Tbsp. minced onion
1/4 cup chopped black olives

Combine all ingredients thoroughly and chill in refrigerator for 20–30 minutes. Remove from refrigerator and roll into a ball.

Step Two:

3/4 cup chopped walnuts
4 sprigs fresh parsley
crackers

Roll cheese ball in nuts and wrap in plastic wrap. Chill until ready to use. To serve, place ball in center of plate, tuck parsley sprigs under edges of ball, and ring plate with crackers.

Chutney and Ham Stuffed Mushrooms

1 hour, 20 minutes

Step One:

10 large mushrooms, stems removed
juice of 1/2 lemon
1/2 cup chopped ham
1 Tbsp. Dijon mustard
1 Tbsp. minced, fig-based chutney
1 rounded Tbsp. sour cream
1 rounded Tbsp. mayonnaise
1 tsp. white vinegar
1 tsp. minced onion
4 sprigs fresh parsley

Sprinkle mushroom caps with lemon juice. Combine remaining ingredients, except parsley, and fill caps. Chill 1 hour. To serve, place caps on plate and tuck parsley around caps.

Cheese Canapés

Step One:

4–5 slices baguette, cut 1/2" thick
1/4 cup Roquefort or blue cheese,
  room temperature
1 tsp. crushed rosemary
1–2 tsp. light olive oil

Preheat broiler to 500°F. Arrange baguette slices in a single layer on a baking sheet. Spread cheese over each baguette slice. Dust with rosemary and lightly drizzle with olive oil.

Step Two:

4–5 slices baguette, cut 1/2" thick
1/4 cup feta cheese
1/2–1 tsp. caraway seeds
1/2 tsp. light olive oil

Arrange baguette slices in a single layer on a baking sheet. Spread cheese over baguette slices. Sprinkle 3–5 caraway seeds over each baguette and drizzle lightly with oil.

Step Three:

red grape clusters

Broil both sets of canapés until cheese is bubbly. Serve immediately on a warm plate garnished with grape clusters.

Bourbon Balls

2 hours, 15 minutes

Step One:

1/4 lb. country sausage
1 cup bourbon
1 cup chili sauce
1 cup firmly packed brown sugar

Preheat oven to 350°F. Roll sausage into bite-size balls. Combine remaining ingredients in oven-proof dish and stir until sugar dissolves. Place sausage balls in dish, cover, and bake for 2 hours.

Step Two:

4–5 sprigs fresh parsley

Remove bourbon balls from sauce to plate. Garnish with parsley and serve with toothpicks.

Spinach Balls

Step One:

1 10-oz. pkg. frozen chopped
   spinach, thawed and squeezed dry
1 cup herbed bread crumbs
1/2 cup freshly grated Parmesan
1/4 cup butter, melted
1/2 small leek, minced
2 eggs
pinch nutmeg

Combine all ingredients and mix well. Shape into bite-size balls. (At this point, the balls may be covered and refrigerated until ready to bake.) Preheat oven to 350°F. Set balls on ungreased baking sheet and bake until golden (10–15 minutes).

Step Two:

3 Tbsp. Dijon mustard
2 egg yolks
2 Tbsp. minced leek
pinch marjoram
2 Tbsp. fresh lemon juice

In blender or food processor, combine all ingredients and mix until creamy.

Step Three:

3/4 cup light olive oil
1/2 cup whipping cream
1 1/2 Tbsp. rinsed capers

With blender or food processor running, add oil to sauce in a thin, steady stream. Add cream and capers; blend well. Pour sauce into small bowl, center on serving tray, and surround with spinach balls.

Artichoke Nibbles

Step One:

2 14-oz. jars marinated artichoke
  crowns, chopped and marinade
  from 1 jar reserved
1 leek, chopped
1 clove garlic, minced

Preheat oven to 325°F. Drain marinade from one jar of artichoke crowns into fry pan. Heat over medium flame. Add leek and garlic. Sauté until limp.

Step Two:

3 eggs
1/4 cup fine bread crumbs
salt and pepper to taste
1/8 tsp. oregano
1/8 tsp. basil
1/8 tsp. Tabasco sauce
1 1/2 cups grated Cheddar cheese
2 tsp. minced fresh parsley
3–4 sprigs fresh parsley

Blend eggs, bread crumbs, and seasonings. Add cheese and parsley; mix well. Add artichokes and leek mixture. Blend well. Pour into shallow, greased baking dish. Bake 30 minutes. Cool slightly and cut into bite-size squares. Arrange on serving tray with parsley sprigs for garnish.

TO HAVE AND TO HOLD
(Salads and Soups)

Your salad can be as provocative as your entrée, whether served as the introduction or the conclusion of your meal. It should delight the eye of your Epicurean mate, suggesting the uniqueness of the hours that lie ahead. This can be a simple accomplishment on your part, yet dazzle your lifetime lover with your attention to detail. The subtle nuances are best expressed by an uninhibited spirit. We offer the following suggestions only as a guide to basic composition—be original and let your creative juices flow!

Leaf Us Alone   **45 minutes**

Spinach Salad with Egg and Bacon Garnish

Step One:

1 clove garlic, slivered
1/4 cup light olive oil
4 slices bacon

Put garlic and oil in bowl and let stand for 45 minutes. Fry bacon until crisp. Drain on paper towels. Crumble bacon.

Step Two:

2 eggs

Put eggs in small saucepan. Cover with water 1" higher than eggs. Bring rapidly to boil. Take pan off heat and let stand 20 minutes to hard-boil eggs. Drain and run under cold water. Peel eggs and chop coarsely.

Step Three:

2 Tbsp. red wine vinegar
2 Tbsp. lemon juice
2 Tbsp. freshly grated Parmesan
  cheese
1/4 tsp. salt
freshly ground pepper to taste

Combine vinegar, lemon juice, cheese, salt, and pepper in bowl. Discard garlic from oil. Whisk oil into bowl in a thin stream (or using food processor, with machine running, add oil in thin stream).

Step Four:

8 oz. fresh spinach, washed and torn
  into bite-size pieces

Toss spinach with dressing from Step Three in bowl until well coated. Divide between 2 salad plates. Sprinkle eggs over spinach. Sprinkle bacon over all.

Garden of Eden

Apple, Almond, and Cranberry Salad

Step One:

1/3 cup mayonnaise (preferably
  Best Foods/Hellman's®)
2 tsp. sugar
2 tsp. lemon juice

Combine all ingredients in a medium bowl, stirring until well blended.

Step Two:

2 medium Red Delicious apples,
  cored and diced
2 ribs celery, thinly sliced
1/3 cup sliced almonds
1/3 cup dried cranberries

Fold all ingredients into dressing until thoroughly coated. Serve immediately or refrigerate until ready to serve.

True Love Leaves

Pear and Avocado Salad with Pear Dressing

Step One:

3 green onions, minced
1 Comice pear, peeled, cored,
  and diced
2 Tbsp. red wine vinegar
1/4 tsp. salt
1/4 tsp. freshly ground pepper
1/4 cup light olive oil

Put onions and pears in food processor and process until smooth. Add vinegar, salt, and pepper. With processor running, add oil in slow, steady stream until smoothly blended.

Step Two:

1 bunch Red Leaf lettuce
3 Comice pears, peeled and cored
3 avocados, peeled and pitted

Arrange lettuce on chilled plates. Slice avocados and pears into thin slices. Alternating pear and avocado slices, fan fruit on top of lettuce. Drizzle with dressing.

Aphrodisia Salad

Mint Scented Orzo Salad with Currants and Pecans

Step One:

1/2 cup light olive oil
2 Tbsp. cider vinegar
1 clove garlic
1 tsp. salt
1 tsp. pepper
1/4 tsp. ground cloves
1/2 tsp. turmeric
pinch saffron (optional)
1 cup loosely packed fresh mint
    leaves

Put all ingredients in food processor and turn machine off and on in short bursts until well blended.

Step Two:

1 12-oz. pkg. orzo (pasta)
1 red pepper, halved and seeded
1/4 cup chopped fresh chives
1 cup coarsely chopped pecans
1 cup currants
2–4 Red Leaf or Romaine lettuce
    leaves

Cook orzo according to package directions. Meanwhile, carefully roast pepper under broiler, turning frequently. When charred, put pepper in paper bag and fold top over tightly. Allow to steam 10 minutes. Drain orzo and spoon into bowl. Stir in chives, pecans, and currants. Scrape and discard charred skin from peppers, chop and add to bowl. Stir in dressing until well blended. Arrange lettuce leaves on salad plates. Top with orzo and serve.

Crab Bisque

Step One:

3/4 cup butter
3/4 cup flour

In heavy stock pot, make a roux by melting butter, whisking in flour, and cooking slowly, stirring often, until golden brown. This takes about 20 minutes.

Step Two:

3 Tbsp. tomato paste
1 large yellow onion, minced
2 ribs celery, minced
1/2 cup minced green onions
4 cloves garlic, minced
2/3 cup finely chopped green bell pepper

Whisk tomato paste into roux. Add vegetables and cook until very tender.

Step Three:

4 16-oz. cans chicken broth
3 Tbsp. chopped fresh parsley
1 Tbsp. Worcestershire sauce
1 bay leaf
1 Tbsp. chopped fresh thyme,
   or 1 tsp. dry thyme
1/8 tsp. white pepper
1 tsp. ketchup
1 lb. crabmeat from freshly cooked crabs

Slowly whisk in stock. Add remaining ingredients and simmer, covered, over low heat for 40 minutes.

Gingered Butternut Squash Soup

30 minutes

Step One:

2 Tbsp. butter
3 cloves garlic, minced
1/2 cup minced onion
3/4 tsp. minced fresh ginger root
1 medium butternut squash, peeled
   and seeded
2 10-oz. cans beef broth
1 1/2 Tbsp. sherry
pinch nutmeg
salt and pepper to taste

Melt butter in large soup pot. Sauté garlic, onion, and ginger until tender. Cut squash into 1/2" slices. Add to pot, along with remaining ingredients. Bring to a boil and simmer 15–20 minutes. Purée in food processor or blender. Serve in warm bowls.

Heart and Sole

45 minutes

This will fillet your heart and soul with passion.

Fillet of Sole in Tarragon Butter

Step One:

2 Tbsp. butter
3/4 cup sliced mushrooms
1 small onion, chopped

Melt butter in large fry pan and sauté mushrooms and onion for 5 minutes.

Step Two:

1 lb. fillet of sole, patted dry
   with paper towels
1/4 cup vermouth
2 Tbsp. butter
1 tsp. tarragon
salt and pepper to taste

Preheat oven to 350°F. Lightly grease 2 au gratin dishes. Arrange fillets in dishes. Pour vermouth over fish and dot with butter. Season with salt, pepper, and tarragon. Spoon mushroom mélange over fish, cover with foil, and bake for 35 minutes.

Undress Rehearsals

Chutney and Ham Stuffed Mushrooms

To Have and to Hold

True Love Leaves

Unbridaled Passions

Heart and Sole

Over the Threshold

Brussels Sprouts and Red Grapes in Almond Butter

Wine

Chenin Blanc

Suite Surrender

The doorway to pleasure will open tonight!

Fillet of Sole with White Grapes

Step One:

1 Tbsp. butter
3 large mushrooms, sliced
1 cup seedless green grapes
1/4 cup sour cream
1/4 cup mayonnaise
1 tsp. lemon juice

Melt butter in small pan over low heat. Sauté mushrooms 3–5 minutes. Add grapes and heat through, stirring gently. Add remaining ingredients, stirring until blended.

Step Two:

1 lb. fillet of sole, patted dry with
   paper towels

Preheat oven to 325°F. Place fillets in greased au gratin dishes. Spoon sauce from Step One over fillets. Cover with foil and bake for 20 minutes.

SUGGESTED MENU

Undress Rehearsals

*Chutney and Ham
Stuffed Mushrooms*

To Have and to Hold

True Love Leaves

Unbridaled Passions

♥ *Suite Surrender*

Over the Threshold

Broccoli in Lemon Sauce

Wine

Riesling

Sneak-a-Peek Snapper

40 minutes

Most women think it is better to be looked over than overlooked. Live up to her expectations and sneak a peek!

Snapper in Caper Cream Sauce

Step One:

1/4 cup clam juice
1/4 cup dry white wine
1/2 cup whipping cream
1/2 tsp. lemon juice
2-3 drops soy sauce

Preheat oven to 400°F. In a small saucepan, combine clam juice and wine. Boil over high flame until reduced to 1/4 cup (approximately 5 minutes). Add remaining ingredients and continue to boil, stirring occasionally, until sauce is reduced to 1/3 cup (approximately 10 minutes). Keep warm.

Step Two:

butter
2 snapper fillets
salt to taste
2 Tbsp. butter, cut into pieces

Butter 2 large pieces of foil. Lay fillets on foil, sprinkle with salt, and dot with butter. Fold and seal foil packets. Place on baking sheet and bake for 12 minutes.

Step Three:

1 tsp. capers, drained
several large leaves Red Leaf lettuce
lemon slices

Add capers to sauce. Place lettuce leaves on plates. Remove snapper from foil and place on lettuce. Nap with sauce and garnish with lemon.

SUGGESTED MENU

Undress Rehearsals

Artichoke Nibbles

To Have and to Hold

Crab Bisque

Unbridaled Passions

♥Sneak-a-Peek Snapper

Over the Threshold

Creamed Spinach

Wine

Sauvignon Blanc

♥ *Makin' Whoopee*

If you've got the inclination, I'll provide the motivation!

Salmon Steaks with Artichoke Hearts

Step One:

1 large salmon steak
pinch dill
salt and pepper to taste

Cut salmon steak in half and lay each half in a separate au gratin dish. Season with dill, salt, and pepper.

Step Two:

1 15-oz. can new potatoes, drained
1 14-oz. jar artichoke hearts

Preheat oven to 400°F. Arrange 2–3 potatoes on one side of each piece of fish. Drain artichoke marinade evenly over fish and potatoes. Reserve hearts. Bake for 10–12 minutes.

Step Three:

artichoke hearts from Step Two
2 sprigs fresh dill (or parsley)
2 lemon pinwheel slices, split from one edge of peel to center of pinwheel and twisted

Garnish fish and potatoes with artichoke hearts and dill. Garnish with a lemon twist on top of each piece of fish.

SUGGESTED MENU

Undress Rehearsals

Cheese Canapés

To Have and to Hold

Crab Bisque

Unbridaled Passions

♥ Makin' Whoopee

Over the Threshold

Scalloped Mushrooms and Almonds

Wine

Chardonnay

Runaway Lovers

With a flick of the wrist, our tryst took a twist, now all that's left to do is "the kiss."

Angel Hair Pasta with Smoked Salmon

Step One:

1 red onion, minced
1/2 cup chopped leek
1 clove garlic, minced
3 Tbsp. butter
1/2 cup dry white wine
1/2 cup chicken stock
1/4 cup whipping cream
2 Tbsp. chopped fresh chives
salt and freshly ground pepper to taste

In fry pan over medium heat, sauté onion, leek, and garlic in butter until tender. Blend wine and stock into onion mixture. Raise heat to medium-high and bring mixture to a simmer. Cook 2–3 minutes. Lower heat and add cream and chives. Season with salt and freshly ground pepper.

Step Two:

1 lb. angel hair pasta
2 Tbsp. butter
3–4 oz. fresh smoked salmon
2 tsp. chopped fresh chives

Cook pasta according to package directions, until al dente. Drain. Toss pasta with sauce and butter. Gently toss in smoked salmon. Sprinkle with chives and serve.

Undress Rehearsals

Escargot in Caps

To Have and to Hold

Leaf Us Alone

Unbridaled Passions

Runaway Lovers

Over the Threshold

Broccoli in Lemon Sauce

Wine

Chardonnay

♥ Maiden Voyage

Christen the evening with this one and the rest of the night will be smooth sailing!

Scallops in White Wine

Step One:

1 lb. scallops, cut into bite-size pieces
1/4 cup flour
1/4 cup butter

Shake scallops and flour in a plastic bag until scallops are evenly coated. Melt butter in fry pan over medium heat and lightly brown scallops.

Step Two:

1/2 cup butter
1 small white onion, minced
1/2 lb. mushrooms, sliced
1 Tbsp. minced garlic
1 tsp. salt
1/2 tsp. white pepper
1 Tbsp. lemon juice
1 cup white wine

Melt butter over medium heat in a clean fry pan. Sauté onion for 5 minutes. Add mushrooms and garlic. Season with salt and pepper. Continue to sauté for 4 minutes. Add scallops, lemon juice, and wine. Simmer 4 minutes or until heated through.

Step Three:

2 Tbsp. minced fresh parsley
lemon wedges

Remove scallops to warm au gratin dishes. Garnish with a sprinkle of parsley and lemon wedges. Serve immediately.

*SUGGESTED
MENU*

Undress Rehearsals

Artichoke Nibbles

To Have and to Hold

Leaf Us Alone

Unbridaled Passions

♥*Maiden Voyage*

Over the Threshold

*Scalloped Mushrooms
and Almonds*

Wine

Chenin Blanc

♥ Sea Nymph Mania

Show him what kind of sea nymph you really are. If you don't have a beach, suggest the hot tub after dinner!

Scallops in Madeira Cream

Step One:
2 Tbsp. butter
1 Tbsp. olive oil
2 Tbsp. flour
3/4 lb. fresh ocean scallops

Preheat oven to 350°F. Melt butter and oil in fry pan over medium-high heat. Put flour in plastic bag and add scallops, shaking until lightly coated. Add scallops to pan and sauté until golden and just firm. Transfer scallops to warmed plate, cover loosely, and keep warm.

Step Two:
2 Tbsp. pine nuts, shelled

Meanwhile, toast pine nuts in oven until lightly browned, stirring occasionally.

Step Three:
2 Tbsp. minced leeks
1/2 cup Madeira
3/4 cup whipping cream
2 Tbsp. brandy
1 tsp. fresh lemon juice
pinch nutmeg

Add leeks to fry pan and sauté 1–2 minutes. Add Madeira and simmer until liquid is reduced by half. Add cream and whisk until slightly thickened. Reduce flame to low and add remaining ingredients. Return scallops to pan and heat through.

Step Four:
1 bunch spinach, washed and
   stems removed
paprika

Divide spinach leaves into 2 au gratin dishes (or 1 serving dish), top with scallops and sauce. Sprinkle with pine nuts and paprika. Serve immediately.

SUGGESTED MENU

Undress Rehearsals

Spinach Balls

To Have and to Hold

Leaf Us Alone

Unbridaled Passions

♥ Sea Nymph Mania

Over the Threshold

Scalloped Mushrooms and Almonds

Wine

Sauvignon Blanc

♥ Insatiable

1 hour, 40 minutes

Too much of a good thing can be wonderful.

Mushroom and Crab Stuffed Seashells with Béchamel Sauce

Step One:

3 Tbsp. butter
1/2 onion, minced
1 clove garlic, minced
6–8 medium mushrooms, chopped
2 Tbsp. minced fresh parsley
1 Tbsp. chopped fresh thyme
1 10-oz. pkg. frozen chopped
   spinach, thawed and squeezed dry
crabmeat from 1 freshly cooked crab
freshly ground pepper to taste
1 egg, slightly beaten

Preheat oven to 350°F. Melt butter over medium heat and sauté vegetables and herbs until tender. Stir in spinach and crab. Season with pepper and heat through. Spoon into bowl, cool slightly, and blend in egg.

Step Two:

3 Tbsp. butter
1/4 cup flour
1 cup lowfat milk
1 cup whipping cream
1 Tbsp. chopped fresh parsley
1 Tbsp. chopped fresh thyme

Melt butter in fry pan, whisk in flour, and cook over medium heat until golden brown. Whisk in milk and cream. Bring to a simmer. Stir until thickened. Add herbs.

Step Three:

16 oz. jumbo seashell pasta

Cook pasta according to package directions until al dente. Drain and run under cold water. Drain thoroughly. Spoon a little sauce into baking dish to coat bottom. Stuff seashells with crab mixture, set into baking dish, and ladle remaining sauce over seashells. Bake for 30 minutes.

SUGGESTED MENU

Undress Rehearsals

Cheese Canapés

To Have and to Hold

True Love Leaves

Unbridaled Passions

♥ *Insatiable*

Over the Threshold

Ginger Glazed Carrots

Wine

Chenin Blanc

A Decadent Duo

. . . is what we will be, I'll indulge you tonight and let you please me!

Crab and Ham Croutons with Mornay Sauce

Step One:

2 Tbsp. butter
2 Tbsp. minced leek
2 Tbsp. flour
salt and pepper to taste
pinch nutmeg
2/3 cup milk
1/2 cup half-and-half
2 Tbsp. dry white wine
1/4 cup grated Swiss cheese
2 Tbsp. grated Parmesan

Melt butter over medium-low flame and sauté leek until transparent. Turn flame to low and add flour, whisking constantly for 2 minutes. Add seasonings, milk, and half-and-half. Whisk until sauce thickens. Add wine and cheeses, whisking until sauce is smooth and not too thick (add half-and-half to thin, if needed). Keep warm.

Step Two:

2 slices white bread, crusts removed
2 Tbsp. butter
4 thin slices ham

In fry pan, melt butter over medium flame and brown bread lightly on both sides. Place bread in warmed au gratin dishes (or serving platter) and top with 2 ham slices each.

Step Three:

1 1/2 Tbsp. butter
1/4–1/2 lb. lump crab meat
salt and pepper to taste
2 Tbsp. chopped fresh chives or
   minced fresh parsley

Melt butter in fry pan, add crab, season to taste, and sauté until heated through. Divide the crab over the ham and nap with sauce from Step One. Garnish with chopped chives or minced parsley.

SUGGESTED MENU

Undress Rehearsals

Chutney and Ham Stuffed Mushrooms

To Have and to Hold

True Love Leaves

Unbridaled Passions

A Decadent Duo

Over the Threshold

Brussels Sprouts with Red Grapes in Almond Butter

Wine

Chenin Blanc

♥*I Do*

. . . want to unveil all your charms, but I promise to wait until after the wedding.

Crab Pizza

Step One:

1 bunch fresh chives, chopped
2 Tbsp. minced fresh dill
1/2 cup mayonnaise
3 tsp. fresh lemon juice
3/4 cup grated mozzarella, Monterey
   Jack, or Swiss cheese
crabmeat from 1 freshly cooked crab

Preheat oven to 450°F. Combine chives, dill, mayonnaise, and lemon juice in bowl and blend well. Stir in cheese. Gently fold in crabmeat.

Step Two:

1 medium ready-made pizza crust
   (such as Boboli)

Spread crab mixture evenly on pizza crust. Bake for 10 minutes. Remove from oven and let stand a few minutes prior to cutting into wedges.

SUGGESTED MENU

Undress Rehearsals

Artichoke Nibbles

To Have and to Hold

True Love Leaves

Unbridaled Passions

♥*I Do*

Wine

Chardonnay

♥ Mon Petit Affair

The best things come in small packages.

Shrimp, Black Bean, and Nectarine Salad with Jalapeño Vinaigrette

Step One:

1 jalapeño pepper

Using tongs, roast pepper over open flame or under broiler until charred and blistered. Place pepper in a paper bag, fold top tightly, and steam pepper for 10 minutes. Scrape off and discard charred skin and mince pepper.

Step Two:

1/4 cup light olive oil
juice of 1 lime (about 1 1/2 Tbsp.)
zest of 1 lime
2 Tbsp. chopped fresh cilantro
1 Tbsp. chopped fresh chives
salt and freshly ground pepper to taste

In small bowl, whisk jalapeño with above ingredients until well blended.

Step Three:

1/2 lemon
10 peppercorns
1 bay leaf
1 lb. shrimp, shelled and deveined
1 15-oz. can black beans
1 large nectarine, pitted and sliced
   in wedges
8 oz. mixed salad greens
4 sprigs fresh cilantro
freshly ground pepper to taste

Fill a dutch oven with 4 quarts water; add lemon, peppercorns, and bay leaf. Bring to a boil. Add shrimp. As shrimp begin to turn orange, remove immediately to large bowl. Add black beans, nectarine, and half of the dressing. Toss gently. Add remaining dressing to greens and toss. Divide greens between 2 plates. Top with shrimp and nectarines; toss lightly. Garnish with sprigs of cilantro and serve with freshly ground pepper.

SUGGESTED MENU

Undress Rehearsals

Chutney and Ham Stuffed Mushrooms

To Have and to Hold

Crab Bisque

Unbridaled Passions

♥Mon Petit Affair

Wine

Riesling

♥Poulet It Again with Me

50 minutes

Romance and intrigue are the keys!

Grilled Vegetable and Chicken Salad with Herbed Feta Cheese

Step One:

1 large red bell pepper, halved and seeded

1 large green bell pepper, halved and seeded

Using tongs, roast peppers over open flame or under broiler until charred and blistered. Place in paper bag and fold top over tightly. Allow peppers to steam for 10–15 minutes.

Step Two:

6 Tbsp. light olive oil

2 Tbsp. balsamic vinegar

1 Tbsp. cider vinegar

freshly ground pepper to taste

salt to taste

Blend all ingredients in small bowl.

Step Three:

3 small, yellow crookneck squash, cut diagonally into 1" chunks

1/4 lb. large mushrooms, cleaned and stems removed

1 large red onion, sliced into 6–8 wedges

Bring grill to medium heat. Place all vegetables in single layer on platter or baking sheet and brush with marinade. Grill vegetables, brushing with marinade, until just cooked through, about 6 minutes. Scrape and discard charred skin from peppers and add them to grill to reheat. Slice into 1" strips.

Step Four:

2 boneless, skinless chicken breasts

Flatten breasts slightly with mallet. Cut into irregular 1 1/2" x 1 1/2" pieces. Place on plate and brush with marinade. As vegetables come off grill, add chicken and cook until springy to touch, about 7 minutes.

Step Five:

1/2 lb. mixed salad greens

4 oz. herbed feta cheese, crumbled

2 Tbsp. chopped fresh chives

Toss greens with remaining marinade and divide onto warm plates. Top with chicken and vegetables. Sprinkle with feta and chives.

Undress Rehearsals

Cheese Canapés

To Have and to Hold

Butternut Squash Soup

Unbridaled Passions

Poulet It Again with Me

Wine

Sauvignon Blanc

Romantic Rendezvous

A romantic rendezvous can happen any time, any place—be spontaneous.

Chicken, Cranberry, and Gorgonzola Salad with Orange Raspberry Dressing

Step One:

2 boneless, skinless chicken breasts
3 Tbsp. vegetable oil
1/2 tsp. paprika
1/2 tsp. garlic salt
1/2 tsp. poultry seasoning
juice of 1/2 lemon

Preheat oven to 350°F. Brush chicken with oil and lay on baking sheet. Sprinkle with herbs and squeeze lemon juice over breasts. Bake 40 minutes. Let cool and slice diagonally into thin strips. Chill.

Step Two:

2 Tbsp. raspberry vinegar
1 Tbsp. frozen orange juice
   concentrate
6 Tbsp. light olive oil

Combine all ingredients in a serving cruet or jar and shake well.

Step Three:

1 head Romaine lettuce, washed
   and torn into bite-size pieces
1/2 cup coarsely chopped walnuts
1/2 cup dried cranberries
3 oz. gorgonzola, crumbled

In large bowl, toss lettuce, walnuts, and cranberries with just enough dressing to coat. Divide onto 2 chilled plates. Top with chicken, then gorgonzola. Sprinkle with remaining dressing and serve.

Undress Rehearsals

Cream Cheese Ball

To Have and to Hold

Butternut Squash Soup

Unbridaled Passions

♥Romantic Rendezvous

Wine

Chenin Blanc

♥ Obsession

I'm obsessed, you're the best, let me put you to the test!

Chicken in Orange Sauce

Step One:

1 3-lb. (or bigger) chicken, cut
   into serving pieces
1/4 cup butter
1 cup sliced mushrooms

Brown chicken in butter over medium heat. Remove to a casserole. Add mushrooms to pan and sauté 3–5 minutes. Scatter mushrooms over chicken.

Step Two:

2 Tbsp. flour
1 1/4 cups orange juice
2 Tbsp. firmly packed brown sugar
1 tsp. salt
1/2 tsp. ground ginger
1 tsp. dry mustard

Preheat oven to 350°F. Turn heat to low and slowly whisk in flour (you may need to alternate flour and orange juice to avoid lumps). Add remaining ingredients and turn heat to medium, stirring constantly until thickened. Pour over chicken and bake for 45 minutes, basting frequently.

Step Three:

1 11-oz. can mandarin oranges,
   drained
 2 Tbsp. chopped fresh parsley

Remove chicken and mushrooms to 2 au gratin dishes, arrange orange sections on top, and sprinkle with parsley.

SUGGESTED MENU

Undress Rehearsals

Bourbon Balls

To Have and to Hold

True Love Leaves

Unbridaled Passions

♥*Obsession*

Over the Threshold

Honey Glazed Acorn Squash

Wine

Gewürztraminer

Provocative Proposal

Don't just tempt me . . . make me an offer I can't refuse!

Chicken Breasts with Avocado-Cheese Topping

Step One:

2 chicken breast halves, skinned
   and boned
1/2 cup flour
1 tsp. salt
1/2 tsp. pepper
2 Tbsp. butter

Preheat oven to 350°F. Combine flour and seasonings in large plastic bag, add chicken, and shake to coat. Melt butter in large fry pan over medium flame. Add chicken and sauté until golden on both sides. Remove to warm plate, cover, and keep warm.

Step Two:

2 Tbsp. butter
1/4 cup chopped onion
1 clove garlic, minced
4 mushrooms, sliced
2 Tbsp. flour
3/4 cup white wine
1/4 cup chicken broth
1 avocado, peeled and mashed
3/4 cup Monterey Jack cheese

Add butter to fry pan and sauté onion, garlic, and mushrooms until softened. Whisk in flour, wine, and broth. Cook, stirring occasionally, for 5 minutes. Add avocado and 1/2 cup cheese; blend well.

Step Three:

Place breasts in warmed au gratin dishes and top with avocado mixture. Sprinkle with remaining cheese and bake 10 minutes, or until chicken is cooked through.

SUGGESTED MENU

Undress Rehearsals

Artichoke Nibbles

To Have and to Hold

Aphrodisia Salad

Unbridaled Passions

Provocative Proposal

Over the Threshold

Creamed Spinach

Wine

Chenin Blanc

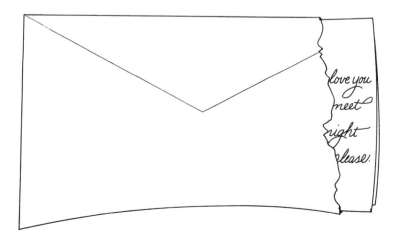

Tonight's the Night!

We'll be dynamite!

Mediterranean Breast of Chicken

Step One:

3 Tbsp. olive oil
1 Tbsp. butter
1 small onion, minced
1 14 1/2-oz. can chopped, peeled
   tomatoes
1/4 cup tomato juice
1/4 cup Marsala
1/4 tsp. coriander
1/4 tsp. fennel seed
1/4 tsp. crushed bay leaf
1/2 tsp. basil
1/2 tsp. oregano
1/2 tsp. thyme
pinch orange peel
minced fresh parsley

Heat oil and butter in large fry pan over medium heat, add onion, and sauté 5 minutes. Stir in remaining ingredients, except parsley, and simmer 1 hour. Remove pan from heat, stir in parsley, and set aside. Start Step Two 15 minutes prior to end of cooking time.

Step Two:

3 Tbsp. butter
2–3 chicken breasts
5–6 Tbsp. freshly grated Parmesan

Preheat broiler to 500°F. Heat butter in a 10" fry pan. Add chicken breasts and sauté 5–8 minutes per side (or until done). Transfer breasts to au gratin dishes, spoon sauce over breasts, and sprinkle with Parmesan. Put under broiler until cheese bubbles, then serve.

SUGGESTED MENU

Undress Rehearsals

Artichoke Nibbles

To Have and to Hold

Leaf Us Alone

Unbridaled Passions

Tonight's the Night

Over the Threshold

Broccoli in Lemon Sauce

Wine

Chardonnay

Hanky Panky

. . . in the beginning, is sure to keep your lover grinning!

Chicken Breasts Stuffed with Prosciutto and Mozzarella

Step One:

2 chicken breast halves, skinned,
   boned, and pounded lightly
1 clove garlic, halved
2 thin slices prosciutto
2–4 thin slices mozzarella
2 Tbsp. seasoned bread crumbs

Preheat oven to 350°F. Lightly grease small baking dish. Rub chicken breasts with garlic. Discard garlic. Lay 1 slice prosciutto over each breast, top with 1 or 2 slices mozzarella. Sprinkle bread crumbs over each breast. Roll, starting at broad end, and secure with tooth-picks. Place rolls in baking dish.

Step Two:

2 Tbsp. dry sherry
2 Tbsp. butter
salt and pepper to taste
1 Tbsp. minced fresh parsley

Melt butter in small saucepan over low flame; blend in sherry. Pour over chicken and season with salt and pepper. Bake 20–25 minutes. Place on warmed plates, sprinkle with parsley, and serve.

SUGGESTED MENU

Undress Rehearsals

Hot 'n' Sweet

To Have and to Hold

Crab Bisque

Unbridaled Passions

Hanky Panky

Over the Threshold

*Ham Wrapped Asparagus
in Cream Sauce*

Wine

Chenin Blanc

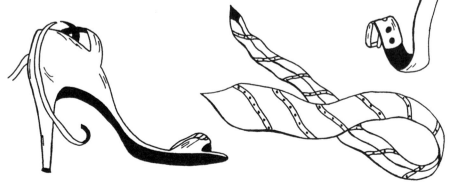

Adam's Sweet Demise

. . . could lead to your own, if you're willing to share a rib with your honey!

Short Ribs of Beef in Raisin Sauce

Step One:

1 lb. boneless beef short ribs
2 Tbsp. shortening
1/2 tsp. salt
1/4 tsp. pepper
1 medium onion, quartered

In deep skillet or dutch oven, brown ribs in shortening and pour off drippings. Season with salt and pepper. Add onion.

Step Two:

1/2 cup firmly packed brown sugar
1 tsp. dry mustard
1/2 cup raisins
1 Tbsp. flour
2 Tbsp. white vinegar
1/4 tsp. grated lemon peel
1 bay leaf
1 1/2 cups water

Combine all ingredients in a small saucepan and bring to boil. Pour over ribs. Cover and simmer on low heat for 2 hours. Remove ribs from sauce, place on serving dish or au gratin dishes, and keep warm in low oven.

Step Three:

2 Tbsp. flour
1/4–1/2 cup hot water
2 sprigs fresh parsley

Shake flour and water in jar. Whisk into sauce. Turn heat to medium and stir until thickened. Remove bay leaf, pour sauce over ribs, and garnish with parsley.

SUGGESTED MENU

Undress Rehearsals

Artichoke Nibbles

To Have and to Hold

Garden of Eden

Unbridaled Passions

Adam's Sweet Demise

Over the Threshold

Honey Glazed Acorn Squash

Wine

Gewürztraminer

♥Get Me to the Church on Thyme 1 hour, 45 minutes

Your perfect timing will keep the wedding bells chiming!

Beef in Wine and Herb Sauce

Step One:

1/4 cup flour
1 lb. lean stew meat, cut into
   bite-size cubes
1 onion, finely chopped
1 clove garlic, minced
3 Tbsp. vegetable oil

Add flour and beef to plastic bag and shake. In large fry pan over medium heat, sauté onion and garlic in oil for 5 minutes. Add beef and brown on all sides.

Step Two:

1 16-oz. can beef broth
1/2 tsp. thyme
1/4 tsp. pepper
1 tsp. oregano
1 tsp. basil
1 bay leaf

Stir all ingredients into fry pan, loosening bits from bottom of pan. Cover and simmer over low heat for 1 hour.

Step Three:

1 cup sliced carrots
8–10 mushroom caps
1/4 cup chopped fresh parsley
1/2 cup burgundy
2 cups cooked noodles, buttered
   and sprinkled with parsley

Add carrots and mushrooms and continue to cook 30 minutes. At end of cooking time, stir in parsley and wine. Heat through for 5 minutes. Serve in au gratin dishes over noodles.

SUGGESTED MENU

Undress Rehearsals

Escargot in Caps

To Have and to Hold

Butternut Squash Soup

Unbridaled Passions

♥ *Get Me to the Church on Thyme*

Over the Threshold

Scalloped Mushrooms and Almonds

Wine

Zinfandel

♥ Sharing Passions

I Worcestershire my love with you.

Dijon and Cognac Beef Stew

Step One:

1 3-oz. block salt pork, rind removed and reserved, remainder diced

1 large onion, chopped

3 shallots, chopped

Cook diced salt pork in heavy skillet over medium heat until golden. Remove with slotted spoon to dutch oven. Add onion and shallot to fry pan and brown over high heat. Remove to dutch oven with slotted spoon.

Step Two:

1/2 cup flour

1 lb. lean stew meat, cut into bite-size pieces

1–2 Tbsp. butter

Shake flour and beef in plastic bag until coated evenly. Add beef to fry pan and brown well on all sides (do not let cubes touch, or they will steam instead of brown). Transfer beef to dutch oven.

Step Three:

1/4 cup cognac

2 cups beef stock

1 Tbsp. Dijon mustard

pork rind from Step One

1/2 tsp. Worcestershire

2 large carrots, cut into bite-size pieces

Pour cognac in fry pan and cook over medium heat until a glaze of liquid is all that remains. Stir in beef stock and bring to boil. Stir in Dijon and pour mixture into dutch oven. Add pork rind. Bring to simmer, cover loosely, and cook 2 hours. Add carrots 30 minutes prior to end of cooking time.

Step Four:

2 Tbsp. butter

8–10 small mushrooms

1/4 cup burgundy

Bring stew to simmer. Heat butter in fry pan, add mushrooms, and brown well. Add wine and boil 20 seconds. Stir into stew and simmer 5 more minutes.

SUGGESTED MENU

Undress Rehearsals

Cheese Canapés

To Have and to Hold

Crab Bisque

Unbridaled Passions

♥ *Sharing Passions*

Over the Threshold

Brandied Sweet Potatoes

Wine

Merlot

♥ *Licensed For Love*

Now that we're "legal," there are no holds barred!

Meatballs in Wine and Herb Sauce

Step One:

1 lb. lean ground beef
1 tsp. salt
1/4 tsp. pepper
1 tsp. fines herbes
1/2 tsp. marjoram
1/4 tsp. rosemary
1 Tbsp. butter

Thoroughly mix meat and seasonings. Shape into 1" balls and brown evenly in butter.

Step Two:

3 Tbsp. brandy

Heat brandy in small pan until edges start to bubble, pour over beef and carefully ignite (do not swish pan, alcohol will burn out and flame will die within a few seconds). When flame dies, remove beef to bowl.

Step Three:

8 oz. small whole mushrooms
8 oz. small white onions, peeled

Add mushrooms to pan and sauté 5 minutes, then remove to bowl. Repeat process with onions and remove.

Step Four:

2 Tbsp. flour
1/2 cup canned beef broth
1 cup burgundy
1/2 cup port
2 Tbsp. tomato paste
1 bay leaf
2 cups cooked noodles, buttered
  and tossed with parsley

Stir flour into drippings with whisk. Add liquids slowly; blend well. Add remaining ingredients and stir until thickened. Simmer 8 minutes. Add beef, onions, and mushrooms. Cover and simmer 20 minutes, stirring occasionally. Serve in au gratin dishes over noodles.

MARRIAGE LICENSE

SUGGESTED MENU

Undress Rehearsals

Cream Cheese Ball

To Have and to Hold

Butternut Squash

Unbridaled Passions

♥ *Licensed for Love*

Over the Threshold

Creamed Spinach

Wine

Zinfandel

Romantic Rehearsal

They say that practice makes perfect . . . let's practice again tonight!

Veal Rolls in White Wine Sauce

Step One:

2 strips bacon, fried and crumbled

1 Tbsp. minced fresh parsley

1 clove garlic, minced

1 cup cooked wild rice (or fresh bread crumbs)

1 egg

1 lb. thin veal fillets (or chicken breasts)

Mix bacon, parsley, garlic, rice, and egg together. Spoon mixture onto veal slices and roll up tightly. Secure with thread or toothpicks.

Step Two:

2 Tbsp. butter

1 Tbsp. flour

2/3 cup chicken broth

2/3 cup white wine

salt and pepper to taste

Melt butter in large fry pan. Add veal rolls and brown quickly over medium heat. Remove rolls to a dish. Add flour to pan and whisk until smooth. Blend in remaining ingredients and bring to a boil. Return rolls to pan, cover, and simmer over low heat for 30 minutes.

Step Three:

1 1/2 cups sliced mushrooms

1 firm tomato, quartered

3–4 sprigs fresh parsley

Add mushrooms and tomato to the pan. Continue cooking for 30 minutes. Serve in individual au gratin dishes and garnish with sprigs of parsley.

SUGGESTED MENU

Undress Rehearsals

Cream Cheese Ball

To Have and to Hold

Leaf Us Alone

Unbridaled Passions

Romantic Rehearsal

Over the Threshold

*Ham Wrapped Asparagus
in Cream Sauce*

Wine

Merlot

Boudoir Fantasy

I'll tell you mine, if you'll tell me yours!

Veal Nuggets in Brandied Raisin Sauce

Step One:

2 Tbsp. butter
1 lb. boned veal shoulder, cubed
1/2 cup brandy
1/2 cup raisins

Melt butter in large fry pan and brown veal. Heat 1/4 cup brandy in small pan and ignite; carefully pour over veal. When flame dies, remove veal to bowl with slotted spoon. Meanwhile, put raisins in remaining brandy to soak.

Step Two:

2 Tbsp. butter
1/4 cup onion, minced
3 Tbsp. flour
1 cup strong coffee
1/2 cup chicken broth

Melt butter in same fry pan and sauté onion over medium heat for 3 minutes. Remove from heat and whisk in flour, coffee, and broth until blended. Remove raisins from brandy and add brandy to sauce. Return to heat and boil, stirring until thickened. Add veal and raisins. Cover and simmer 1 1/2 hours.

Step Three:

2 cups cooked noodles
1/2 cup sour cream
1 tsp. tarragon
3–4 sprigs fresh parsley

Divide noodles between 2 au gratin dishes. Remove veal from sauce and place in au gratin dishes. Stir sour cream and tarragon into sauce. Heat through, but do not boil. Spoon sauce over veal and garnish with parsley sprigs.

SUGGESTED MENU

Undress Rehearsals

Spinach Balls

To Have and to Hold

True Love Leaves

Unbridaled Passions

Boudoir Fantasy

Over the Threshold

Brussels Sprouts and Red Grapes in Almond Butter

Wine

Gamay Beaujolais

Hot Engagements

Let's engage in the hot pursuit of passion tonight!

Pork Chops in Sauce Dijon

Step One:

2–3 boneless pork loin chops,
   well-trimmed
2 Tbsp. flour
salt and pepper to taste
2 Tbsp. butter
1/4 cup white wine
1 Tbsp. lemon juice

Dry chops with paper towels. Shake flour, salt, and pepper in plastic bag. Add chops and shake to coat. Melt butter in large fry pan and brown chops over medium heat 8–10 minutes per side. Add wine and juice. Cover and simmer on low heat 1 hour.

Step Two:

1 1/2 Tbsp. flour
1 cup cream
2 Tbsp. Dijon mustard
dash cayenne

3–4 sprigs fresh parsley

Remove chops to au gratin dishes and keep warm. Whisk flour into pan drippings (after removing any lumps of fat), add cream, mustard, and cayenne. Bring mixture to boil, stirring constantly. Pour sauce over chops and garnish with parsley.

SUGGESTED MENU

Undress Rehearsals

Hot 'n' Sweet

To Have and to Hold

Garden of Eden Salad

Unbridaled Passions

Hot Engagements

Over the Threshold

Brandied Sweet Potatoes

Wine

Cabernet Sauvignon

The Folly of Eve

Adam didn't mind at all when she put it to him this way . . .

Sherried Pork Chops and Apples

Step One:

2–3 boneless pork loin chops,
   well-trimmed
1 Tbsp. vegetable oil

Preheat oven to 325°F. Brown chops in oil over medium heat for 8–10 minutes per side.

Step Two:

2 apples, cored and sliced
1/2 tsp. cinnamon
1/4 cup firmly packed brown sugar
2 Tbsp. butter
3/4 cup sherry

Arrange pork chops in greased casserole. Layer apples over chops and sprinkle with cinnamon and brown sugar. Dot with butter and pour sherry over all. Cover and bake for 1 1/2 hours.

Step Three:

3–4 sprigs fresh parsley

Arrange chops in 2 au gratin dishes, place apple slices over chops, and spoon sauce over all. Garnish with parsley sprigs.

SUGGESTED MENU

Undress Rehearsals

Chutney and Ham Stuffed Mushrooms

To Have and to Hold

Aphrodisia Salad

Unbridaled Passions

The Folly of Eve

Over the Threshold

Ginger Glazed Carrots

Wine

Chardonnay

♥ Cupid's Conquest

1 hour, 25 minutes

The Romans called him **Cupid,** *the Greeks called him* **Eros.** *Whatever you call him, passion is his game.*

Braised Pork Chops with Peaches

Step One:

2–3 boneless pork loin chops, well-trimmed
salt and pepper to taste
1 cup sliced green onions
1 10 3/4-oz. can cream of chicken soup
1/4 cup white wine
3/4 cup chicken broth
1 1/2 tsp. prepared mustard
syrup from 1 8-oz. can sliced peaches, peaches reserved

Season chops with salt and pepper. Brown in a lightly greased pan over medium heat 8–10 minutes per side. Add onion and continue cooking until tender. Stir in soup, wine, broth, mustard, and peach syrup. Bring to boil, cover, and simmer 45 minutes.

Step Two:

3–4 sprigs fresh parsley

Add peaches from Step One and heat through. Place chops in au gratin dishes and arrange peaches on top. Pour sauce over all and garnish with parsley.

SUGGESTED MENU

Undress Rehearsals

Bourbon Balls

To Have and to Hold

Aphrodisia Salad

Unbridaled Passions

♥ *Cupid's Conquest*

Over the Threshold

Brandied Sweet Potatoes

Wine

Riesling

Passion Potion

A little potion will give her the notion and set the evening into motion!

Linguine with Hot Walnut, Blue Cheese, and Prosciutto Sauce

Step One:

1/3 cup light olive oil
1 clove garlic, minced

Heat oil in small pan. Add garlic and sauté until limp. Remove pan from heat. Pour oil and garlic into mixing bowl.

Step Two:

2/3 cup chopped fresh parsley
1 cup coarsely chopped walnuts
2 Tbsp. minced fresh rosemary
6 slices prosciutto, chopped (or
    4 oz. chopped smoky ham)
1/2 tsp. freshly ground black pepper
4 oz. blue cheese, crumbled

Fold all ingredients into oil and let stand 2 hours, allowing flavors to blend.

Step Three:

8–12 oz. uncooked linguine

Bring a large pot of salted water to boil. Add linguine, stirring to separate. Bring to a boil, turn heat down, and simmer until al dente, 10–14 minutes. Drain, add linguine to dressing, and toss gently, allowing cheese to just begin melting. Serve immediately.

SUGGESTED MENU

Undress Rehearsals

Cheese Canapés

To Have and to Hold

Leaf Us Alone

Unbridaled Passions

Passion Potion

Over the Threshold

Broccoli in Lemon Sauce

Wine

Sauvignon Blanc

♥ Making Sparks Fly

Now that we're married, we can get carried away when we spark in the dark!

Warm Black and White Bean Salad with Grilled Italian Sausage

Step One:

1 lb. Italian sausage

Preheat grill to medium heat. Pierce sausage in several places with fork. Grill sausage about 4 minutes per side, or until done. Place on plate, cover, and keep warm.

Step Two:

1 bay leaf
10 peppercorns
1/2 onion
3 ribs celery, cut into 2" pieces
1 carrot, cut into 1" pieces
1 15-oz. can black beans, rinsed
  and drained
1 15-oz. can white beans, rinsed
  and drained

Fill 3 qt. saucepan half full with water. Add all ingredients, except beans, and bring to a simmer. Add beans and simmer 5 minutes.

Step Three:

1 vidalia or maui onion, minced
1 roasted red bell pepper, diced
1/2 cup chopped fresh parsley
2 Tbsp. chopped fresh thyme
3 Tbsp. red wine vinegar
1/4 cup light olive oil

Combine vegetables, herbs, and vinegar. Let stand a few minutes. Add oil in a slow, steady stream, whisking constantly until well blended. Slice sausages diagonally, reserving juices. Add juices to dressing. Drain beans and toss with dressing.

Step Four:

4–6 leaves Romaine or Red Leaf
  lettuce

Fan 2–3 lettuce leaves on warm plates. Mound beans at base of leaves. Arrange sliced sausage on plates. Serve immediately.

SUGGESTED MENU

Undress Rehearsals

Hot 'n' Sweet

To Have and to Hold

Crab Bisque

Unbridaled Passions

♥Making Sparks Fly

Wine

Gewürztraminer

Fan the Flames

For as Zsa Zsa Gabor said, "Husbands are like fires, they go out if unattended."

Roasted Peppers, Hot Sausage, and Herbed Pasta with Asiago

Step One:

2 yellow bell peppers, halved
 and seeded
2 red bell peppers, halved
 and seeded

Roast peppers, using tongs, over open flame or under broiler. Place peppers in paper bag, fold top tightly, and steam 10 minutes. Scrape and discard charred skin from peppers and cut into short 1" x 1/4" ribbons.

Step Two:

1 lb. mushrooms, sliced
3 Tbsp. light olive oil
2 cloves garlic, minced
Salt and pepper to taste
1/2 cup chopped fresh parsley
1 Tbsp. chopped fresh thyme
1/4 cup dry white wine

Sauté mushrooms in olive oil until golden brown. Add garlic and sauté 1 minute. Season with salt and pepper and add herbs and wine. Cook 2 minutes. Scrape into large shallow pasta dish. Toss in peppers.

Step Three:

1 lb. kielbasa, casing removed and
 sausage sliced diagonally
1 lb. pasta, such as farfalle,
 mostaccioli, or radiatore
1/2 cup grated Asiago or
 Parmesan cheese
French bread

Brown kielbasa in fry pan over medium heat about 4 minutes per side. Drain on towels and add to dish. Meanwhile, cook pasta according to package directions until al dente. Drain, reserving about 1/4 cup pasta liquid. Add pasta to bowl. Moisten with reserved pasta liquid and gently toss. Sprinkle with Asiago and serve with crusty French bread.

Undress Rehearsals

Spinach Balls

To Have and to Hold

Leaf Us Alone

Unbridaled Passions

Fan the Flames

Over the Threshold

Honey Glazed Acorn Squash

Wine

Pinot Noir

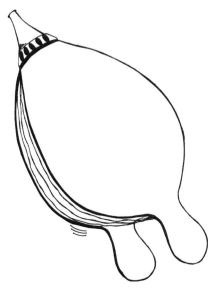

Undercover Passions

We've only just begun . . . but I've lost count already!

Rabbit in White Wine Sauce

Step One:

3 Tbsp. butter

1 rabbit, cut into serving pieces

Melt butter in large fry pan and brown rabbit slowly over medium-low heat.

Step Two:

1 clove garlic, chopped

2 medium onions, sliced

1 rounded Tbsp. flour

1 cup white wine

2 cups chicken broth

6 cherry tomatoes

Remove rabbit from pan. Add garlic and onion to pan and sauté 5 minutes. Whisk in flour and cook over low heat until browned. Add wine and broth. Bring to boil. Add tomatoes.

Step Three:

1/2 tsp. thyme

2 bay leaves

2 Tbsp. chopped fresh parsley

1/2 tsp. salt

1/2 tsp. pepper

4–5 mushroom caps

3–4 sprigs fresh parsley

Add spices and seasonings to sauce and return rabbit to pan. Liquid should just cover rabbit; add more broth if needed. Simmer 1 1/2 to 2 hours. Add mushrooms during last 20 minutes of cooking time. Arrange rabbit in individual au gratin dishes, pour sauce over rabbit, and garnish with parsley sprigs.

SUGGESTED MENU

Undress Rehearsals

Cream Cheese Balls

To Have and to Hold

Crab Bisque

Unbridaled Passions

♥Undercover Passions

Over the Threshold

Honey Glazed Acorn Squash

Wine

Chardonnay

♥ Lusty Lambkins

Wool ewe be mine?

Lamb Stew

Step One:

1 1/2 lb. lamb, cubed
2 small onions, quartered
2 large carrots, sliced
1 15-oz. can new potatoes
1 bay leaf
1 Tbsp. lemon juice
3 cups water
1 cup sliced mushrooms
salt and pepper to taste

Place all ingredients, except mushrooms, in dutch oven. Bring to boil, cover, and simmer 1 1/2–2 hours. Add mushrooms during last 20 minutes of cooking time. Remove lamb and vegetables to covered serving dish and keep warm.

Step Two:

3 Tbsp. butter
6 Tbsp. flour

Reduce cooking liquid to about 2 1/2 cups by boiling and stirring. In separate saucepan, melt butter and add flour while stirring constantly. Add the reduced liquid to saucepan slowly, stirring constantly. Simmer 5 minutes.

Step Three:

1 egg yolk
1/2 cup heavy cream

Blend yolk and cream. Add a little sauce from pan and blend. Stir this mixture into the saucepan and heat through. Pour sauce over meat and vegetables. Serve immediately.

SUGGESTED MENU

Undress Rehearsals

Spinach Balls

To Have and to Hold

Butternut Squash Soup

Unbridaled Passions

♥Lusty Lambkins

Over the Threshold

Broccoli in Lemon Sauce

Wine

Cabernet Sauvignon

♥ 1,001 Nights

Be like Scheherazade; keep him coming back for more!

Lamb Shish Kebab

Step One:

6–8 Brussels sprouts, cooked
8–10 fresh whole mushrooms
8–10 cherry tomatoes
8 small white boiling onions, peeled
1 boneless lamb shoulder, cubed
1/2 lb. bacon

Place all ingredients except bacon in large bowl or rectangular dish. Bring small saucepan of water to boil over high flame. Add bacon and turn flame to medium heat. Cook 10 minutes. Remove and add to lamb mixture.

Step Two:

1 cup vegetable oil
1/4 cup lemon juice
2 cloves garlic, crushed
1/4 tsp. thyme

Combine all ingredients and pour over vegetables and meats. Marinate at least 1 hour.

Step Three:

Starting with bacon, thread meat and vegetables on skewers, interlacing bacon over and under each piece. Grill over medium-high heat, turning and basting frequently for even browning, 15–30 minutes or until lamb is cooked through as desired.

SUGGESTED MENU

Undress Rehearsals

Cream Cheese Balls

To Have and to Hold

Aphrodisia Salad

Unbridaled Passions

♥ *1,001 Nights*

Over the Threshold

Honey Glazed Acorn Squash

Wine

Pinot Noir

Scalloped Mushrooms and Almonds   25 minutes

Step One:

1/2 cup slivered almonds

Place almonds in a small fry pan over lowest heat and toast, stirring constantly. Remove from pan and set aside.

Step Two:

1 cup sliced mushrooms
1/2 cup butter
1 cup half-and-half

Sauté mushrooms in butter until tender, approximately 5 minutes. Add half-and-half and bring to simmer.

Step Three:

2 Tbsp. flour
1/4 cup water
salt and pepper to taste
2 Tbsp. chopped fresh parsley
2 sprigs fresh parsley

Shake flour and water in a jar until well blended. Add to pan and stir constantly until thickened. Add almonds, salt, and pepper. Sprinkle parsley over all and spoon into small au gratin dishes. Garnish with sprigs of parsley. (This may be kept warm in the oven. When ready to serve, add milk to sauce if needed.)

Honey Glazed Acorn Squash   45 minutes

Step One:

1 medium acorn squash

Preheat oven to 350°F. Cut squash in half and remove seeds. Place squash cut side down in a baking dish. Bake for 20–30 minutes or until squash is tender.

Step Two:

1/4 cup butter, melted
1/4 tsp. ground ginger
1/4 tsp. cinnamon
1/4 tsp. salt
1/4 cup honey
1/4 cup chopped walnuts

Combine all ingredients, blending well. Turn squash right-side up in baking dish and fill cavities with sauce. Be sure to spoon some sauce over tops and sides of squash. Bake for an additional 15 minutes. Baste once.

Brandied Sweet Potatoes

25 minutes

Step One:

1/2 cup chopped walnuts
1/4 cup butter

Sauté walnuts in butter until lightly toasted. Remove walnuts from pan.

Step Two:

1/2 cup firmly packed brown sugar
1/2 tsp. salt
1/2 cup orange juice (juice from canned peaches or apricots may be substituted)
1/2 tsp. grated orange peel

Add all ingredients to pan and bring to boil for 3–4 minutes. Reduce heat and return walnuts to pan.

Step Three:

1 15-oz. can sweet potatoes, cut into bite-size pieces

Add sweet potatoes to sauce and stir to coat. Heat thoroughly and transfer to serving bowl or small au gratin dishes.

Step Four:

1/4 cup brandy

Heat brandy in small pan until bubbles form around edge of brandy. Pour over sweet potatoes and ignite carefully. Serve flaming.

Ginger Glazed Carrots

15 minutes

Step One:

3-4 carrots, sliced into coins

Steam carrots until tender.

Step Two:

1/4 cup butter
1/4 cup honey
1/2 tsp. ground ginger
1 Tbsp. minced fresh parsley

In small saucepan, melt butter; stir in honey and ginger. Add carrots and stir to coat. Toss with parsley and serve.

Broccoli in Lemon Sauce

25 minutes

Step One:

1/2 bunch fresh broccoli,
  cut into serving pieces

Steam broccoli until tender.

Step Two:

2 Tbsp. butter
1 Tbsp. flour
1/2 cup milk

Melt butter in small fry pan and gradually whisk in flour. Slowly add milk, stirring constantly to avoid lumps.

Step Three:

1 tsp. grated lemon peel
1 Tbsp. lemon juice
1/4 tsp. ground ginger
1/4 tsp. salt

Gradually add lemon peel and lemon juice, then add ginger and salt. Stir until blended well.

Step Four:

lemon pinwheel slices, split from
  one edge of peel to center of
  pinwheel and twisted

Transfer broccoli to small au gratin or serving dish and spoon sauce over top. Garnish with lemon twists.

Ham Wrapped Asparagus in Cream Sauce

40 minutes

Step One:

8–10 spears asparagus, trimmed to 7"
2 slices ham, 2" x 6" x 1/8" in size

Steam asparagus until just tender. Divide asparagus into two servings. Wrap a slice of ham around middle of spears and lay seam side down in baking dish.

Step Two:

1 large egg
3/4 cup whipping cream
2 Tbsp. grated Swiss cheese
2 Tbsp. grated Parmesan cheese

Preheat oven to 350°F. Blend egg and cream. Pour over asparagus bundles. Sprinkle with cheeses. Bake 25–30 minutes, or until cream is set and cheeses are golden brown.

Creamed Spinach

Step One:

2 Tbsp. butter
2 Tbsp. flour
1 1/4 cups milk
salt and pepper to taste

Melt butter in fry pan over medium-low heat. Whisk in flour and cook 2–3 minutes. Whisk in milk and bring to boil. Add salt and pepper and remove from heat. Set aside 1/2 cup of cream sauce and reserve the rest for another recipe.

Step Two:

1 3-oz. block salt pork, diced and
   rind discarded
1/4 cup minced leek
1 10-oz. package frozen spinach,
   thawed and squeezed dry
salt and pepper to taste
1/2 cream sauce from Step One

In fry pan over medium heat, sauté salt pork until browned. Add leek and sauté until translucent. Add spinach, salt, and pepper, stirring until heated through. Add cream sauce, cover, and cook over low flame 20–25 minutes, stirring occasionally.

Brussels Sprouts and Red Grapes in Almond Butter

20 minutes

Step One:

1/4 cup sliced almonds

Toast almonds in small fry pan over medium heat until lightly browned. Remove from pan and set aside.

Step Two:

10 oz. Brussels sprouts, trimmed
1 Tbsp. butter
1 cup seedless Red Flame grapes

Steam Brussels sprouts until crisp-tender. Melt butter in fry pan over medium heat. Sauté sprouts and grapes 2–3 minutes. Toss with almonds and serve.

SUBJECT INDEX

Lamb

RECIPE INDEX